# Joe Root:

From Prodigy to Cricket Legend

Jeffrey E. Woods

**Copyright © Jeffrey E. Woods,2024**

All rights reserved. No part of this publication may be reproduced or transmitted in any form or by any means including photocopying, recording or other electronic or mechanical methods without the prior written permission of the publisher except in the case of brief quotations embodied in critical reviews and certain other non-commercial uses permitted by copyright law.

# TABLE OF CONTENTS

INTRODUCTION

Chapter 1: Childhood

Chapter 2: Ascent to Notoriety

Chapter 3: England's Premier

Chapter 4: Groundbreaking Acts

Chapter 5: Years of Captaincy

Chapter 6: Special Moments

Chapter 7: Records and Milestones

Chapter 8: Obstacles and Reversals

Chapter 9: Implications and Legacy

CONCLUSION

# INTRODUCTION

Few names are as well-known in the cricket world as Joe Root. Root's career is a tribute to the strength of perseverance, hard work, and natural skill. He began as a remarkable young batsman and is now regarded as one of the best players of his generation. Over the course of a ten-year career, Root has been a stalwart in English cricket, receiving universal praise for his technical prowess, situational awareness, and unrelenting dedication to the game he loves.

Root's narrative is not limited to his achievements in sports. It's a tale of fervor, tenacity, and a deep-seated ambition to excel. It is the tale of a young Sheffield kid who dreamed big and put forth a lot of effort to make those aspirations come true. An inspiring tale of a young guy who persevered through many obstacles and disappointments without ever losing sight of his objectives. An inspiring tale of a real champion whose extraordinary talent, steadfast commitment, and unquenchable passion for the game have inspired countless admirers worldwide.

The amazing life and career of Joe Root are examined in this book, from his early years spent playing cricket with his brother Billy to his current standing as a cricket icon. We look at the pivotal events that shaped his path, the difficulties he has encountered, and the victories he has attained. We explore his career's highs and lows, his moments of overwhelming joy and heartbreaking loss. We examine the individuals and locations that have influenced him, the events that have changed him, and the principles that have led him.

We are given a unique perspective on Root's motivations, what makes him successful, and what makes him stand out from his colleagues through exclusive interviews and insider knowledge. We hear from his teammates, coaches, friends, and family—those who know him best. We acquire a better comprehension of his advantages and disadvantages, his drives and aspirations, and his fears and dreams.

This book is perfect for anyone who enjoys a good story or is an ardent cricket fan. Come along as we examine the amazing life story of the real cricket legend, Joe Root. A narrative that will enthrall, encourage, and inspire you. A narrative that will transport you on an exciting, triumphant, and discovering journey.

# Chapter 1: Childhood

The narrative of Joe Root starts on December 30, 1990, in the peaceful Sheffield suburb of Dore. Joe Root, the son of Matt and Helen Root, started playing cricket at a young age. Matt, his father, was a club cricket player for Sheffield Collegiate Cricket Club, a prestigious team that has sent out a number of famous players. Don Root, his grandpa, was also quite active in Yorkshire cricket. Joe's passion for cricket was cultivated in this cricketing atmosphere.

Joe was surrounded by crickets as a child. The sound of leather against willow, the sight of verdant fields, and the companionship of cricket matches occupy his earliest recollections. His future in the sport was set up by these events. Joe has a natural knack for cricket from an early age. He would frequently lose hours playing cricket in the garden with his younger brother Billy, who would also go on to play professionally.

Collegiate Cricket Club Sheffield

At Sheffield Collegiate Cricket Club, where his father played, Joe got his official cricket education. The club, which places a high priority on the development of young people, gave Joe the ideal setting in which to refine his abilities. He rose through the ranks fast, participating in teams for different age groups and winning over peers and coaches with his poise and technique at the crease. Kevin Sharp, one of Joe's first coaches at Sheffield Collegiate, remembers a young Joe who was not only gifted but also extraordinarily committed and industrious. Sharp observed that Joe maintained his composure under duress, a quality that would ultimately come to define him. Joe's innate talent and hard ethic, along with the supportive atmosphere of the club, created the conditions for his quick progress.

The Education and Equilibrium Act

Joe was a passionate cricket player, but he was also a fantastic student. He was well-known for his scholastic accomplishments and athletic abilities at Sheffield's King Ecgbert School. Joe had to juggle his cricket responsibilities with his studies, but he did it with style. His ability to maintain high standards in the classroom and on the cricket field often left his professors and coaches in awe. Joe continued to learn outside of the classroom. He carried on with his studies at Worksop College, a cricket-loving institution. Joe's cricket skills developed even more at

Worksop under the direction of knowledgeable instructors. He had the chance to participate in the school's elite cricket program, and it was during this time that his promise as a future professional cricket player started to show.

Family Influence

For Joe, his family was the most important factor in his cricketing growth. His first coach and mentor was his father, Matt, who instilled a strong work ethic and a love for the game in him. Joe would frequently accompany Matt to the nets for extra practice sessions, where Matt would emphasize the value of perseverance and hard effort. Helen, Joe's mother, gave him resolute support and made sure he had everything he needed to follow his cricketing goals. Billy, Joe's younger brother, accompanied him on his cricketing journey constantly. The two brothers pushed one another to enhance their talents over their many hours of cricket play. Joe was able to feel a sense of camaraderie and good competitiveness with Billy, which fueled his enthusiasm for the game even more.

Early Accomplishments and Acknowledgment

Joe's skill was not overlooked. His age-group cricket performances were garnering him attention in local publications by the time he was a teenager. He was compared to some of the greatest players in history due to his ability to score runs on a regular basis and his mature batting style. Selectors and coaches started to take notice, and it was obvious that Joe was going to be awarded higher distinctions.

Joe's acceptance into the Yorkshire Academy, a renowned program created to nurture young cricket players with the potential to play at the top level, was one of his early accomplishments.

Joe trained with some of the top young players in the area and received excellent instruction at the academy. His cricket career was greatly shaped by his time at the Yorkshire Academy, where he gained the knowledge and expertise necessary to succeed in the professional game.

The Choice to Go Professional with Cricket

Joe's decision to play cricket professionally was inevitable as his cricketing journey developed. His accomplishments during his youth and academy years solidified his status as one of the nation's most promising young cricket players. This choice was greatly influenced by his friends, coaches, and family's encouragement and support.

Joe's decision to forgo a university education and devote all of his attention to cricket demonstrated his dedication to the game. Although it was a risky decision, it showed his commitment to achieving the greatest possible success. Ready to leave his mark in professional cricket, Joe started the next chapter of his adventure with the support of his family and the cricket community. Joe Root's formative years serve as a testament to the value of skill, perseverance, and a nurturing environment in attaining achievement. Joe's story, which starts in Sheffield and continues through the Yorkshire Cricket League, is marked by a strong passion for the game and an uncompromising dedication to perfection. The groundwork he put in these early years would pay dividends when he entered the professional ranks, setting the stage for an incredible career that would make him one of cricket's greatest players ever.

## Chapter 2: Ascent to Notoriety

When Joe Root played his first County Championship game for Yorkshire in 2007, his career as a celebrity really took off. He was one of the youngest players to wear the Yorkshire white rose, having only turned 16 years old. His initial outings demonstrated promise, and he quickly became a regular member of the squad.

When Root was given more chances to bat higher in the order in 2010, it was the season that marked his breakthrough. Both selectors and analysts were impressed by his skill, demeanor, and capacity for scoring runs under duress. For any young batter, reaching over 1,000 runs at the conclusion of the season is a noteworthy accomplishment. He was named Yorkshire

Player of the Year for this effort, which speaks volumes about his rising reputation in domestic cricket.

Success for Under-19s and National Attention

Root was chosen for the England Under-19 squad as a result of his success at the national level. He was a member of the team that played in New Zealand during the 2010 ICC Under-19 Cricket World Cup. With his outstanding tournament exploits, Root became one of England's most valuable players, scoring regularly against very good opponents.

In addition to giving him priceless international experience, his time with the England Under-19 team made him known to the national selectors. Root's potential for success at the top level was evident, and his age group and domestic cricket exploits reinforced his claim to be included in the senior England side.

Premier Achievement and the England Lions

Joe Root was unquestionably one of the most talented young batters in English cricket by 2012. His Yorkshire performances kept getting better, and he was always in the top half of the run scorers in the County Championship. His maturity at the crease belied his young age, as he showed an obvious ability to adapt to various formats and conditions.

Because of his performance at home, Root was chosen for the England Lions, the backup squad for the national team. He had the chance to practice and improve his talents against international competition while he was a member of the Lions. His performances with the

Lions were impressive, and his technique and demeanor kept selecting coaches interested.

Test Launch and Initial Achievements

During England's tour of India in December 2012, Joe Root made his eagerly anticipated Test debut. at the fourth Test at Nagpur, an important game for England, he was given his debut. Root's poise and technique were instantly apparent as he helped England win the series 2-1 with 73 runs in his opening innings. His highly acclaimed debut performance signaled the start of a new phase in his career.

After experiencing early success in Test cricket, Root went on to put up strong performances in the series that followed. At his home stadium of Headingley, he made his first Test century against New Zealand in 2013. The innings solidified his spot in the England batting lineup and was a masterpiece in focus and ability. Root was a great asset to England because of his ability to score runs against elite bowlers and in difficult circumstances.

Growth in Cricket's Limited-Overs

Although Joe Root was primarily concerned with Test cricket, he also achieved great success in limited-overs games. He was an important member of England's Twenty20 International (T20I) and One-Day International (ODI) teams because of his versatility and adaptability. After making his ODI debut against India in January 2013, Root became a dependable middle-order batsman.

Root's ability to score runs quickly while staying extremely consistent was a key factor in his limited-overs cricket success. His efforts in important tournaments further increased his reputation, and he was instrumental in several of England's victories. Root's versatility and skill were evident in his ranking as one of the best batsmen in all game forms by 2015.

The Ashes of 2015 and Growing Notoriety

A pivotal occasion in Joe Root's career occurred in the 2015 Ashes series versus Australia. One of cricket's most famous rivalries, the Ashes, offered Root the ideal platform to display his skills. He set the tone for England's campaign early in the series with a magnificent century in the opening Test at Cardiff. England won the series 3-2 thanks in large part to Root's performances, which earned him the title of player of the series.

Root became a cricket superstar with his performance in the 2015 Ashes series. Both analysts and fans praised him for his ability to play well under duress and turn in game-winning performances. England saw a sea change after winning the series, and Root's performances were regarded as essential to the team's comeback.

Becoming a Premier Batsman and Making His Mark

After the 2015 Ashes series, Joe Root carried on his winning ways. He became one of the best batsmen in the world of cricket by scoring runs reliably in both the home and away series. He was a challenging batsman to dismiss due to his technique, focus, and versatility in the field. Root's reputation was further cemented by his performances on difficult international tours, including those in Australia, South Africa, and India.

Root's extraordinary constancy was a defining feature of his ascent to fame. He regularly played vital innings and scored hundreds of runs to help England win. He was a complete batter since he could play aggressively when needed and anchor the innings when necessary. As one of the world's best batters by 2017, Root's name was often discussed with that of other contemporary greats like Virat Kohli, Steve Smith, and Kane Williamson.

Leadership and Persistent Achievement

Alastair Cook was replaced as the England Test team captain in 2017 by Joe Root. Given his stature and performances, it was thought that making Root captain was a natural next step. His ability to motivate his teammates, combined with his tactical skill and calm demeanor, defined his leadership style. England had tremendous victories under Root's leadership, including historic series victories and standout individual performances.

As captain, Root set an exemplary example for the squad, frequently leading them through difficult circumstances and scoring important runs. He remained one of England's most dependable run-scorers, demonstrating a laudable ability to reconcile the demands of captaincy with his batting. England accomplished great things under his direction, and Root's leadership qualities were well-received.

Joe Root's ascent to fame is a result of his skill, diligence, and everlasting commitment to the game. From his early years at Yorkshire to his current status as one of the world's best batsmen,

Root's career has been distinguished by reliable play, outstanding accomplishments, and a steadfast passion for the game of cricket. His leadership abilities and capacity for success across all game formats have elevated him to the status of a living legend in contemporary cricket. Even while Root is still writing fresh chapters in his career, his reputation as one of England's all-time great cricket players is already cemented. His ascent to fame is not only the result of his own talent but also of his dedication to the game and capacity to motivate upcoming cricket players.

# Chapter 3: England's Premier

Joe Root's path to his England debut was the result of many years of perseverance, hard work, and reliable domestic cricket performances. Root has solidified his position as one of the most promising players in English cricket by the end of 2012. His efforts for Yorkshire and the England Lions had proved his potential to thrive at the highest level.

Root was the perfect choice to strengthen the batting order, according to the England selectors, who were eager to add new talent to the squad. His poise, technical skill, and capacity for handling pressure made him a valuable asset to the national team. Cricket fans and the team alike were thrilled and full of optimism when

Root was named in the squad for the Test series against India.

The Choice

Joe Root was included in the England team for the 2012–13 tour of India, which was a difficult task considering the spin-friendly conditions and India's impressive home record. Despite their strong performance in the first three Tests of the series, England still needed to win the series. The selection committee took a risk when they included Root in the fourth and final Test in Nagpur.

Root worked hard to prepare for the Test. He understood how crucial it was to leave a lasting impression with his first season. Both his teammates and the coaching staff were impressed by his concentrated attitude and composed manner during practice. There was a real buzz around his debut, and Root was eager to take advantage of it.

First Game: Nagpur, Fourth Test

On December 13, 2012, Joe Root made his Test debut against India in Nagpur during the fourth Test of the series. He batted at number six and, with England in a tough situation at 119 for 4, walked to the crease. Even though there was a lot of pressure, Root maintained his cool as soon as he assumed responsibility.

Root's first innings was a patient, technical masterclass. Against a formidable Indian bowling attack that featured spinners Pragyan Ojha and Ravichandran Ashwin, he showed impressive maturity for a 21-year-old. Root had remarkable footwork and shot selection as he deftly handled the spin and tempo. His ability to play with soft hands and spin the attack allowed him to form an important connection with Matt Prior.

With 73 runs off 229 balls, Root's innings demonstrated guts and determination. His performance steadied the innings and helped England to a competitive total. His first-inning performance was noteworthy not only for the runs he scored but also for the assurance and confidence he showed under trying circumstances. Commentators and cricket analysts praised his ability to play a methodical innings while absorbing pressure.

Recognition Following Debut

Joe Root's career took a significant turn after his outstanding start. He received praise from his coaches, teammates, and the cricket community for his performance in Nagpur. Alastair Cook, the captain of England, highlighted Root's capacity to withstand pressure while complimenting his maturity and temperament. In addition, the media praised Root's debut and identified him as an English cricket player of the future.

After a draw in the Nagpur Test, England won the series 2-1, their first triumph against India in a Test series since 1984–85. The success of the club was largely due to Root, whose first innings were regarded as a precursor to things to come. His breakthrough performance in international cricket was made possible by the confidence he earned from it.

Change to a Permanent Member of the Team

Joe Root made a great debut and soon established himself as a mainstay in the England squad. His ability to adjust and be versatile made him an invaluable asset in any scenario. Root kept building on his early success, contributing vital innings in the home and away series and scoring runs on a regular basis.

To further highlight his adaptability, Root made his ODI and T20I debuts in 2013 against India and New Zealand, respectively. His versatility and competence were demonstrated by his ability to perform consistently in each format while switching between them with ease. When it came to limited-overs cricket, Root was known for his ability to score runs swiftly and with great regularity.

Initial Test Achievements

Joe Root had a number of noteworthy performances during his early success in Test cricket. He became the youngest Englishman to strike a century at Lord's when he made his first

Test century there during the 2013 Ashes series. His match-winning innings of 180 in the second Test proved that he could play on a major platform. Root's place in the England squad was further solidified by his performance in the Ashes series. He kept up his steady run-scoring and was crucial to England's wins in the next series. One of the most dependable batsmen on the squad, he excelled in difficult situations both domestically and overseas.

Gaining Recognition in Limited-Overs Cricket

Joe Root not only excelled in Test cricket but also became a vital member of England's limited-overs squads. His ability to score runs quickly and adjust to various match scenarios defined his performances in both ODIs and T20Is. Root is considered one of the best batsmen in the world thanks to his steady achievements in limited-overs cricket.

In limited-overs cricket, Root gave one of his best performances in India during the 2016 ICC World Twenty20. Through critical runs and match-winning leadership, he was instrumental in leading England to the championship. During the group stage, his 83-run innings against South Africa stood out in particular because it demonstrated his capacity to pursue big objectives under duress.

Joe Root's career took off after his debut in Nagpur, and he went on to become one of the best batsmen in the world of cricket. It was clear from a distance that he could perform well under pressure and adjust to various situations. The first inning set the standard for a career marked by dependability, tenacity, and a great passion for the game.

In addition to his talent, Root's ascent to fame was also fueled by his commitment, diligence, and the encouragement of his teammates, coaches, and family. His rise from a teenage prodigy in Sheffield to a Test debutant in Nagpur and finally to one of the best batsmen in the world is evidence of his unflinching dedication to perfection.

A journey that would lead him to high heights in international cricket began with Joe Root's England debut, which was a pivotal event in his career. His performance in Nagpur demonstrated his aptitude, his temperament, and his capacity to perform under duress—qualities that would come to define his remarkable career. Even though Root is still making an impact on the cricket world, his debut is still remembered as a pivotal moment that signaled the advent of a great.

# Chapter 4: Groundbreaking Acts

The First Century

Against Australia at Lord's in the second Test of the Ashes series in 2013, Joe Root had one of his most memorable moments. Root's career reached a major turning point in this game as he amassed his first Test century, an innings of 180 runs. In addition to being a personal triumph, this performance was crucial to England's success in the series.

Root's batting performance at Lord's demonstrated both his technical skill and mental fortitude. In the face of a formidable Australian attack spearheaded by Mitchell Starc and Peter Siddle, Root showed incredible forbearance and agility. His innings were marked by a combination of unwavering will and ferocity, as well as classical shot-making and sound technique. His century helped England to a substantial first-inning total that ultimately contributed to their win in the game.

Root's ability to establish himself as one of England's best young batters and a future star in international cricket was demonstrated by this performance.

Sri Lanka's 2014 Series

Joe Root had another outstanding performance early in 2014 while touring Sri Lanka with England. In the first innings of the second Test match of the series, Root amassed an incredible double century, reaching 200 without being out. This particular inning was noteworthy due to its caliber as well as the playing circumstances.

The spin-friendly conditions in Sri Lanka presented a big obstacle, but Root's strategy against spin was excellent. He demonstrated his ability to use the depth of the crease and play both aggressive and defensive shots with equal ease during his innings, which was a masterclass in spin bowling. England was able to secure a victory in the match and achieve a challenging total thanks in large part to Root's performance.

The Ashes Series of 2015

England's victory in the 2015 Ashes series against Australia was greatly influenced by Joe Root's efforts. His 134-run innings that ended the match in the second Test at Lord's was one of his most memorable performances. In a series where everything was on the line, this inning was crucial in helping England tie the score.

Throughout his innings, Root combined good technique with aggressive stroke play. With poise and style, he handled a formidable Australian assault that featured bowlers like Mitchell Starc and Josh Hazlewood. His developing batsmanship was evident in his ability to steady the innings while also picking up speed when necessary. The way Root performed under pressure during an Ashes series was just as noteworthy as the number of runs he scored during the innings.

The ICC World Twenty20 in 2016

Joe Root's batsmanship proved to be even more versatile during the 2016 ICC World Twenty20, which took place in India. During England's campaign, Root was instrumental, scoring 83 runs in a memorable group-stage match against South Africa. His performance demonstrated his ability to perform well in the game's shortest format and was crucial in helping them chase down a challenging target of 230 runs.

Power-hitting and deft placement combined to create a memorable innings for Root, highlighting his versatility in T20 cricket. His World Twenty20 performance demonstrated his ability to perform well under duress and in high-stakes games, solidifying his place as an important member of England's limited-overs squad.

The Ashes Series of 2017–18

Joe Root demonstrated his leadership qualities and batting abilities throughout the 2017–18 Ashes series in Australia. Even though England struggled mightily throughout the series, Root made several significant contributions, most notably a brilliant 142 in the opening Test match in Brisbane. In a contest where England had to contend with a formidable Australian attack, this innings was a demonstration of talent and tenacity.

Root's ability to handle the pace and bounce of Australian conditions was evident throughout his innings at the Gabba. In an otherwise difficult series, his performance gave England a glimpse of optimism. Throughout the series, Root's versatility and ability to produce pivotal performances under duress were on full display.

The Double Centuries of 2021

In 2021, Joe Root achieved a remarkable feat by scoring three double centuries in a single calendar year, a testament to his exceptional form and consistency. His double century against Sri Lanka in Galle, where he scored 228 not out, was a highlight of the series. This innings was typified by Root's ability to bat for lengthy periods, showcasing his endurance and concentration.

Root followed this up with another double century against India at Chennai, where he scored 218 runs. His innings were vital in England achieving a solid total and earning a victory in the Test match. His performances throughout the series were a testament to his brilliance and versatility.

Later in the year, Root achieved a third double-century against Australia in the Ashes series, further confirming his place as one of the world's greatest batters. His 2021 performances demonstrated both his extraordinary form and his capacity to perform under a variety of circumstances.

The Pakistan Test Series in 2022

Joe Root has been a consistently excellent batsman in the 2022 Test series against Pakistan. His remarkable innings of 115 in the opening Test match at Rawalpindi demonstrated his ability to score runs in difficult circumstances. Root's innings were highlighted by his smooth stroke play and his ability to adjust to different sorts of deliveries.

Root's performance in the series was a continuation of his outstanding run of form and reinforced his status as one of the finest Test batters in the world. His expertise and commitment were demonstrated by his ability to perform consistently in a variety of settings and forms.

One of Joe Root's most notable professional moments has been his breakthrough performances. From his maiden Test century at Lord's to his incredible double centuries in 2021, Root has consistently proved his talent, perseverance, and capacity to perform under pressure. His performances in major series and tournaments have not only established him as one of the elite batsmen in world cricket but also showcased his versatility and adaptability across all formats and situations. Root's career is evidence of his perseverance, hard effort, and unshakable devotion to greatness.

# Chapter 5: Years of Captaincy

In February 2017, Joe Root took over as England's Test captain, replacing Alastair Cook. Given Root's reputation as one of England's best batters and his leadership abilities, the appointment was viewed as a logical step. When Root was appointed, the England Test squad was going through a period of change, and his position as captain was considered critical to the team's future development.

Root was known for his tactical skill, calm manner, and emphasis on creating a supportive team environment. Players, coaches, and supporters alike enthusiastically greeted his appointment, viewing him as a player possessing the ideal balance of talent, wisdom, and leadership attributes to steer England through a difficult time.

## The 2017–18 Ashes Series

Joe Root had his first significant test as captain during the Australian Ashes series in 2017–18. With England hoping to recapture the Ashes following a home loss, the series was much anticipated. In difficult circumstances, England faced a formidable Australian team, testing Root's leadership.

Despite England's general struggles in the series, Root showed tenacity and competence. In the first Test in Brisbane, he played a remarkable innings of 142 that demonstrated his resilience under duress. Throughout the entire series, Root's leadership was distinguished by his attempts to uplift and encourage his group despite adversity. Despite England's 4-0 series defeat, Root's leadership and play were viewed as encouraging indicators for the future.

## The Sri Lanka Test Series of 2018–19

When England traveled to Sri Lanka in 2018 for a Test series, the obstacles were different. England's batsmen were put to the test by the spin-friendly conditions, but Root's batting and leadership were crucial to the team's victory. Root led by example early in the series, making a double century in the opening Test at Galle, which was vital in putting England in a commanding position.

The fact that Root could adjust to the circumstances and offer a steady presence at the top of the order was essential to England's 3-0 series win. His strategic approach and ability to lead the team through difficult situations won him recognition for his leadership. The series victory was regarded as a noteworthy accomplishment and evidence of Root's leadership qualities.

The ICC Cricket World Cup in 2019

Although Joe Root's main responsibility was as Test captain, he was also an important member of the England limited-overs team. One of the biggest highlights of England's limited-overs campaign was the 2019 ICC Cricket World Cup, in which Root was instrumental.

England's aggressive and creative batting style was a defining feature of their World Cup campaign. England's run to the final was greatly aided by Root's dependability and ability to anchor the innings. His contributions to England's success during the group stages and elimination rounds were crucial. England won the thrilling Super Over match to emerge winners in the World Cup final against New Zealand. Root made a major impact on England's victory in the World Cup during the competition.

The Ashes Series for 2020–21

The Australian-hosted 2020–21 Ashes series posed yet another significant test for Joe Root's leadership. The series was performed in accordance with stringent COVID-19 protocols, which made the tour much more intricate. England had a mixed record in the series and had to deal with a number of issues, such as injuries and the absence of important players.

A formidable Australian side tested England's ability to compete, putting Root's leadership to the test once more. Despite the difficulties, Root showed resiliency and carried on setting a good example. His remarkable 228-run innings in the fourth Test match in Sydney demonstrated his ability to score runs and stabilize the England batting order. England lost the series 4-0, but Root's teamwork and individual efforts were acknowledged as positive aspects of a difficult series.

Emphasis on Team Culture and Development

Throughout his captaincy, Joe Root placed a great emphasis on fostering a positive team culture and developing young players. His leadership style was defined by a focus on building a supportive and inclusive environment for players. Open communication, building a sense of camaraderie, and enabling players to express themselves were all part of Root's leadership style.

Root's backing for up-and-coming players and his attempts to incorporate them into the squad demonstrated his dedication to nurturing fresh potential. His leadership sought to establish a group that was driven, cohesive, and competitive. One of the main influences on how English cricket would develop in the future was Root's emphasis on team culture and development.

Adaptivity and Resilience

Throughout his time as captain, Joe Root demonstrated resilience and flexibility in the face of a variety of obstacles. Root showed that he could motivate and lead his squad by overcoming obstacles, handling injuries, and adjusting to shifting circumstances. His capacity to remain upbeat and lead the group through challenging times was evidence of his leadership abilities.

Another aspect of Root's leadership style was his openness to change and growth. He was receptive to criticism and always worked to become a better captain. One of his most important leadership qualities was his flexibility in changing tactics and strategies according to the circumstances.

Joe Root's tenure as captain of the England cricket team saw tremendous personal and team improvement during this time. Resilience, flexibility, and a strong focus on team culture and development were characteristics of his leadership. Even though he had difficulties during his time, Root's leadership has had a significant impact on how English cricket has developed. Root's capacity to set a good example, motivate his colleagues, and handle difficult circumstances have all come to characterize his leadership. During his time as captain, he not only demonstrated his ability to lead others but also his dedication to the team and the game. As he plays on, Root's captaincy legacy will be shaped by his commitment, tenacity, and the constructive influence he has had on English cricket.

# Chapter 6: Special Moments

2013's The Maiden Century: Lord's

One of Joe Root's most memorable performances of the 2013 Ashes series was his first-ever Test century at Lord's. A pivotal moment in Root's career, his 180-degree knock demonstrated his ability and poise under duress.

When faced with a potent Australian attack, Root showed remarkable maturity and technique. His inning was marked by traditional stroke play, with deft drives and strong defense. Root's capacity to steadily accumulate wickets and quicken his pace when necessary was essential in establishing England's dominant position. He became known as a rising star in international cricket after his performance at Lord's, which was a turning point in the series.

Galle, 2018: The Double Century

Joe Root made history in the 2018 Test series against Sri Lanka with his double century in the opening Test at Galle. Root achieved an incredible feat of 228 not out, especially considering the difficult spin-friendly conditions.

Root's innings was a spin bowling masterclass. He showed off his superb footwork and ability to counter the Sri Lankan spinners by utilizing the depth of the crease. His innings demonstrated his versatility in adjusting to various forms and conditions, which was essential in England's dominant position in the game. In addition to helping England win the series, Root's double-century solidified his status as one of the best batters in the world.

The Ashes Century of 2015: Who's

During the 2015 Ashes series, Joe Root made history with a career-high 134 in the second Test at Lord's. Considering the series' overall backdrop and the caliber of the opposition, this inning was very noteworthy.

Throughout his innings, Root showed his ability to stave off a difficult Australian attack. He played with style and assurance, fusing powerful strokes with sound technique. His knock was crucial in getting England into a position where they could win the game and ultimately emerged victorious in the series 3-2. Root's performance at Lord's showed his capacity to play well under duress and make a major impact on his team's achievement.

## World Twenty20 ICC 2016: 83 Against South Africa

In a match with a lot on the line, Joe Root's 83-run innings against South Africa during the 2016 ICC World Twenty20 were vital. England had a challenging target of 230 to pursue, and Root's performance proved crucial in leading the side to victory.

Root's ability to strike a balance between aggression and accuracy was evident in his performance. He executed a variety of creative shots with superb timing and placement. His innings demonstrated his ability to succeed in the game's shortest format and was a crucial part of England's victorious chase. England made it to the tournament final thanks in large part to Root's contribution.

Chennai, the 2021 Double Century

During England's Test series against India in early 2021, Joe Root struck a stunning double century in Chennai. One of his career's most memorable performances, his 218-ball innings demonstrated his extraordinary form.

Root played a very skillful and focused innings. On a difficult pitch, he was up against a potent Indian bowling attack and used a blend of patience and aggression in his performance. His innings were essential to England's triumph as they helped them establish a commanding position in the game. Root's performance in Chennai demonstrated his capacity to perform well under demanding circumstances and under duress.

The 115th Test Series in Rawalpindi for 2022

Joe Root's 115-run innings in the opening Test match of the 2022 Test series against Pakistan at Rawalpindi will live in memory. The quality of the innings was important, but so were the circumstances and the overall backdrop of the game.

Throughout his innings, Root demonstrated his versatility and control against the Pakistani bowlers. He showed that he could adjust to various situations by playing a variety of shots. His innings demonstrated his ongoing brilliance as a batsman and contributed significantly to England's commanding position in the game. Root's display in Rawalpindi was evidence of his proficiency and reliability.

The Ashes: 228 in Sydney in 2020–21

Joe Root's 228-run innings in the fourth Test at Sydney during the 2020–21 Ashes series in Australia was a noteworthy effort. In a series where England encountered numerous difficulties, Root's innings was a crucial contribution.

Root's skill and tenacity were evident in his Sydney performance. He played with determination and technique against a potent Australian attack. His innings proved his mettle in difficult circumstances and was a major contributor to England's performance in the game. During his captaincy, Root's knock against Sydney stands out as an example of his ability to set an example for others.

The Century of 2014: Headingley

Joe Root made a spectacular century at Headingley, reaching 154 not out, during the 2014 series against India. Because of its caliber and the setting in which it was played, these innings were noteworthy.

Root's ability to manage difficult conditions and a potent Indian bowling assault was evident in his performance at Headingley. His innings, which were a blend of powerful strokes and sound technique, were essential in putting England in a commanding position. A pivotal point in Root's career, his century at Headingley illustrated his rising reputation as one of England's best batsmen.

A number of standout innings that demonstrated Joe Root's extraordinary talent and capacity to execute under duress have defined his career.

Across a variety of forms and circumstances, Root has continuously produced outstanding performances, from his first century at Lord's to his double hundreds in Chennai and Galle. In addition to being a major factor in England's victories, his innings have demonstrated his talent, tenacity, and versatility as one of the best batsmen in the world.

# Chapter 7: Records and Milestones

Alongside his ascent in the world of international cricket, Joe Root achieved a number of noteworthy feats and records that demonstrated his skill and promise. During the 2013 Ashes series, he became the youngest English batsman to score a century at Lord's, which was one of his early career highlights. In addition to being a noteworthy career achievement, Root's 180 was a major contributing element to England's series win.

Quickest to One Thousand Trials

Joe Root became the first Englishman to reach 1,000 Test runs, which was a noteworthy landmark. In just 21 games, he surpassed Alastair Cook's previous record to reach this milestone. Root's record was a tribute to his early success and promise. His consistency and prodigious run-scoring made him one of the best batsmen in Test cricket.

Maximum Number of Runs in a Year

Joe Root became the first English player to score 1,700 Test runs in a calendar year in 2021, setting a new record for batters in the country. Several noteworthy performances, including multiple double hundreds, were part of his spectacular year. With his accomplishment, Root demonstrated his remarkable form and consistency, capping one of the most prosperous years for an English batsman in Test cricket history.

Maximum Runs in One Test Series

In the 2021 Test series against India, Joe Root made history by becoming the first batsman from England to hit more than 600 runs in a single series. With two double hundreds among his 736 runs in the series, he broke the previous record for most runs scored by an English batsman in a Test series. This accomplishment served as evidence of Root's great form and capacity to deliver reliable performance in the face of formidable resistance.

England's highest test score as a batsman

Joe Root set a record for the greatest Test score by an English batsman in February 2021 when he hit 228 runs in a Chennai match against India.

This inning broke Alastair Cook's previous record and showed that Root could still perform at his best under trying circumstances. His innings demonstrated his extraordinary skill and focus and were crucial to England's victory in the game.

Most Centuries as Captain of England

The record for the most centuries achieved by an England captain is held by Joe Root. One of his greatest qualities as a captain has been his ability to lead the team and score runs on a regular basis. Several of Root's century have been game-winning efforts, and they have greatly aided England's victories while he was captain. His track record as England captain is evidence of both his batting ability and leadership qualities.

Fastest in ODIs to 50, 100, and 150

Joe Root has broken multiple records in One Day Internationals (ODIs), including being the fastest to achieve the 50, 100, and 150 run milestones. He is one of the best batsmen in limited-overs cricket (ODI) because of his ability to score runs fast and perform important innings. Root's performances in One-Day Internationals demonstrate his adaptability to various game forms.

The Most Runs in T20Is Record

Among his accomplishments in Twenty20 Internationals (T20Is) is the record he holds for the most runs an English batsman has scored in T20Is. His success has been largely attributed to his ability to play aggressively and adjust to the fast-paced nature of T20 cricket. Root's T20I record demonstrates his versatility and talent in the game's shortest format.

Maximum Innings Absent a Duck

The longest innings played by an English batsman without being out for a duck has been set by Joe Root. This accomplishment has been made possible in large part by his consistency and innings-building skills. Root's track record demonstrates his ability to focus and stay in form for extended periods of time.

English batsman with highest individual score in T20 Internationals

During the 2016 ICC World Twenty20, Joe Root broke the record for the highest individual score by an English batsman in T20 Internationals when he struck 83 runs against South Africa. This was an important contribution in a high-stakes game that showed he could play well in T20 cricket.

A string of noteworthy releases and accomplishments throughout Joe Root's career attest to his extraordinary talent and dependability. Root has made a name for himself as one of the best batsmen in the world of cricket, breaking records in ODIs and T20Is and becoming the fastest Englishman to 1,000 Test runs. His accomplishments demonstrate his talent, flexibility, and capacity to give his best work in a variety of settings and media.

# Chapter 8: Obstacles and Reversals

The First Difficulties in International Cricket

There were difficulties in Joe Root's path to the top of the international cricket scene. As a young prodigy, Root had to live up to enormous expectations early in his career. From playing cricket at home to playing at the top level, he had to adjust to the faster and more accurate bowling assaults, along with the usual setbacks that come with making a name for oneself.

A frequent problem for many young cricketers, fluctuating form was one of Root's early concerns. Even though he had a great start, there were times when he performed poorly and came under fire from both fans and critics. These difficulties were a part of Root's learning process as he attempted to establish himself in the England squad.

Australia's 2014 Tour

For Joe Root, the Australian Ashes series in 2014–15 presented a formidable task. England had a difficult series as they faced a formidable Australian team. Even while Root had flashes of brilliance, he struggled to produce consistently in the hard Australian climate.

He was unable to keep up with the pace and bounce of the wickets when faced with an intense Australian bowling attack. Root learned a lot during this series since he had to modify his strategy and approach to perform well under trying circumstances. Despite the difficulties,

Root's fortitude and tenacity were clear as he improved his performance to get past these obstacles.

Damage and Form Concerns

Joe Root has experienced form problems and injury concerns throughout his career, which have put his fortitude to the test. His rhythm and consistency have occasionally been affected by injuries that have forced him to miss important matches and trips. Periods of bad form have also been difficult for Root because he had to put in a lot of effort to restore his touch and confidence.

Root's mental toughness and dedication to the game are demonstrated by his ability to bounce back from these losses. His strategy for overcoming setbacks and form problems has included rigorous rehabilitation, fine-tuning, and an emphasis on preserving physical and mental clarity.

## The Ashes Series for 2020–21

Australia's 2020–21 Ashes series provided serious obstacles for England captain Joe Root and his squad. Strict COVID-19 protocols were followed during the series, which increased pressure and interfered with regular activities. England's campaign was made more difficult by a number of problems, including injuries and the unavailability of important players.

Root's management style was tested as the team found it difficult to contend with a formidable Australian opposition. Root's performances, including his innings of 228 in Sydney, were the highlights of the series despite criticism and difficult conditions. His capacity to set a good example and stay composed under duress was crucial to England's performance in the series.

Captaincy and Personal Form in Balance

Joe Root has found it difficult to strike a balance between his duties as captain and keeping up his personal condition. It takes a lot of time, energy, and mental toughness to lead the England Test team, and this can occasionally have an impact on a player's individual performance.

In order to maintain his top-notch batting, Root has had to balance the responsibilities of captaincy. His expertise and commitment are evident in his ability to manage these obligations and still turn in excellent at-bat performances. Finding methods to maintain motivation and focus for both himself and his squad has been Root's strategy for juggling the combined responsibilities of captain and top batter.

Managing Pressure and Criticism

Throughout his career, Joe Root, a well-known player in English cricket, has been under intense scrutiny and criticism. Root has had to deal with the demands and expectations that come with being a professional cricket player, whether they are connected to his performances, his leadership, or his decision-making.

One of Root's most important professional traits has been his ability to take criticism well and remain composed. In order to cope with outside expectations, he has worked on his game, asked for input, and addressed his areas of weakness. His demeanor in the face of criticism is a reflection of his professionalism and dedication to his cricket career.

Rebounds and Adaptability

Throughout his career, Joe Root has made a number of noteworthy returns that attest to his tenacity and resolve. Root has a history of overcoming obstacles and going through slumps to produce powerful comebacks. His mental toughness and devotion to the sport are demonstrated by his ability to bounce back from failures and carry on giving his all.

Technical improvements, increased physical conditioning, and a fresh emphasis on his craft have all been key components of Root's comebacks. One of the most distinctive aspects of his career has been his ability to bounce back from setbacks and maintain his success.

The Double Centuries of 2021

When Joe Root scored three double-hundreds in a single year in 2021, it was one of his greatest career comebacks. This accomplishment was especially notable because it came after years of criticism and difficulties. Root's performances, such as his two century against India and Sri Lanka, showcased his capacity to overcome obstacles and reclaim his best form.

Root's two centuries in 2021 demonstrated his talent, flexibility, and fortitude. His remarkable performances and record-breaking feats were a major contributor to his career comeback and confirmed his place among the top batsmen in the world.

Throughout his career, Joe Root has demonstrated a strong sense of resilience and determination in the face of adversity. From overcoming setbacks in his early career to handling injuries, form problems, and the demands of captaincy, Root has shown an incredible ability to recover and carry on playing at the top level. His resiliency and comebacks serve as evidence of his devotion to the game and his pursuit of cricket greatness.

# Chapter 9: Implications and Legacy

Joe Root has had a significant impact on English cricket, helping to shape the modern era with his outstanding leadership and batting abilities. In addition to establishing new benchmarks for English cricket, his contributions have improved the squad's results abroad. Root is one of the best batters of his generation thanks to his consistency, versatility, and skill.

Root's career has been characterized by an amalgamation of conventional methods and contemporary strategies, mirroring the dynamic character of cricket. His ability to mix creative shots with traditional batting has inspired younger players and helped England win in a variety of formats. Beyond just his stats, Root has had a huge influence in shaping England's Test strategy and guiding the team through important setbacks and victories.

Effect in the role of Captain

Joe Root, the captain of the England Test squad, has been instrumental in establishing the culture and direction of the group. Strategic thinking, team cohesion, and an emphasis on positivity have been hallmarks of his leadership. Under Root's leadership, England has seen both challenging and transitional times, from the highs of winning series to the lows of challenging tours.

Players have commended Root's leadership style for being inclusive and motivating. He has made an effort to establish a welcoming atmosphere where players may flourish and express themselves. The way the England squad plays the game and interacts as a unit has been impacted by his attention on creating a strong team culture and his leadership style.

A Contribution to the Success of England

Joe Root has played a pivotal role in England's achievements in various media. His Test cricket exploits, which have included multiple hundreds and noteworthy innings, have been pivotal to England's victories and series victories. The fact that Root can play well under duress and step up when things count has been crucial to England's success.

Root's adaptability and consistency in limited-overs forms have made him an important member of the England team. His efforts at the 2019 ICC Cricket World Cup demonstrated his capacity to play in crucial games and aid in team success, and they were crucial to England's historic victory.

impact on upcoming cricket players

Young cricket players have benefited greatly from the influence of Joe Root. Aspiring cricketers have found inspiration in his batting strategy, work ethic, and outlook on the game. Root's accomplishments have shown the value of talent, commitment, and flexibility and served as an example for aspiring athletes.

Root's influence has been further enhanced by his participation in grassroots cricket and his readiness to interact with the upcoming generation of cricket players. Through involvement in mentoring programs, coaching clinics, and public appearances, Root has aided in the advancement of young players and the evolution of the game.

Documents and Significant Occurrences

Joe Root's accomplishments and records will always be remembered in cricket history. Root's accomplishments, which include becoming the fastest Englishman to reach 1,000 Test runs and setting records for most runs in a calendar year and most hundreds as England captain, are evidence of his brilliance and dependability.

These milestones have not only demonstrated Root's personal brilliance but also established new standards for upcoming cricket players. His accomplishments are a testament to his commitment to the game and his capacity for sustained peak performance.

Input into Team Dynamics

Joe Root has an impact on team dynamics in addition to his individual performances. The way he leads and interacts with teammates has helped to create a cohesive and happy team atmosphere. Root's emphasis on team spirit and his capacity to cultivate strong relationships within the group has been important in creating a cohesive and effective team.

Root's emphasis on cooperation, communication, and mutual support has contributed to the development of a team environment where players are motivated and feel appreciated. His contributions to team chemistry have established a benchmark for cohesiveness and togetherness within the team and have been crucial to England's victories.

Durable Heritage

In cricket, Joe Root left behind a legacy of impact, leadership, and excellence. His status as one of the game's greatest players has been cemented by his on-field accomplishments, team-building efforts, and impact on the upcoming crop of cricket players. A combination of talent, commitment, and leadership has defined Root's career, and his influence on cricket will endure for many years.

As he plays on, Root's legacy will be determined by his continued contributions to cricket and his part in influencing the game's future. Future generations of cricket players will be motivated and inspired by his legacy because of his influence on English cricket and the game in general.

Joe Root left behind a lasting and diverse legacy in cricket. Root has contributed greatly to cricket, from his outstanding batting displays and leadership to his impact on upcoming players and team chemistry. His career is defined by his records, accomplishments, and beneficial influence on English cricket; these things also guarantee that his legacy will be honored and remembered for many years to come.

# CONCLUSION

As the incredible tale of Joe Root comes to an end, we are left feeling incredibly in awe of and admiring a real cricket icon. Root's journey, which began when he was a remarkable young batsman and continues now as one of the greatest players of his time, is proof of the transformational potential that natural talent, hard effort, and devotion can have.

Root has seen many obstacles and disappointments throughout his career, but he has never lost sight of his objectives. He has consistently worked to better himself and be the best version of himself, remaining modest, grounded, and loyal to who he is. Numerous admirers worldwide have been impressed by his unflinching dedication to perfection, and his legacy will inspire and enthrall upcoming generations of cricket players and sports fans alike.

We are reminded of Root's significant influence on the cricket world as we consider his accomplishments. With his remarkable technical proficiency, creative strokeplay, and unrelenting mental tenacity, he has completely revolutionized and elevated the sport of hitting to new levels. A new generation of cricket players has been motivated by him to aspire to greatness, push the envelope of what's feasible, and follow in his footsteps.

Root's impact goes far beyond his accomplishments on the field. He has taught us the value of tenacity, fortitude, and never giving up on our goals. He has demonstrated to us that greatness is possible if we put in the necessary effort, have perseverance, and are dedicated to perfection. He has served as a reminder that real champions are created via a blend of innate ability, perseverance, and a never-ending quest for perfection.

We are aware that Root's tale is far from done as we look to the future. His incredible talent and steadfast commitment to the sport he loves will only serve to inspire, motivate, and enthrall us. He will never stop innovating, pushing the envelope, and changing with the times to always be one step ahead of the competition.

The life of Joe Root serves as a reminder that real greatness is about more than just accomplishment; it's also about the path we choose to follow. It is about the people we encounter, the adventures we go on, and the life lessons we discover. It is about the battles we win, the barriers we go beyond, and the difficulties we face.

Printed in Great Britain
by Amazon